Complete Horoscope

Gemini 2021

Monthly astrological forecasts for 2021

TATIANA BORSCH

Translated from Russian by Sonja Swenson-Khalchenia
Translation copyright © Coinflow Limited, Cyprus
AstraArt Books is an imprint of Coinflow limited, Cyprus
Published by Coinflow Limited, Cyprus
For queries please contact: tatianaborsch@yahoo.com

ISBN: 978-9925-579-34-1 (print)
ISBN: 978-9925-579-35-8 (ebook)

Contents

2021 ~ Birth of a new world

Based on the events of this year, my 2020 predictions, which were published on my website and in *SWAAY* magazine, are coming true (I write this article in summer 2020). We are bearing witness to an era of change; the world is teetering on the brink, and everything we thought was permanent and unshakable has turned out not to be. What else lies ahead?

It is impossible to separate the events of 2020 and 2021. These are years of major shifts, with an effect on each country, each home, and each individual. 2020's developments will continue in 2021, and there is simply no equivalent in modern history. It's safe to say that mankind has not experienced these kinds of changes in a very long time.

Major astrological events during this period are:

The first conjunction of Saturn and Jupiter in the air element will take place in Aquarius. This extremely significant event will literally take place as 2020 becomes 2021- on December 25, 2020.

This means the dawn of the Age of Aquarius, which almost everyone has heard about.

The Age of Aquarius is very long, lasting 2,160 years. It is determined by the Earth's shift from one axis to another. This transition period from one age to another can last a long time. Many astrologists believe that it will last at least 100 years. The last 20 years have been turbulent – they were vital preparation for the adoption of new rules for a new era.

All of this means that 2020 is the last year of the outgoing Age of Pisces, and 2021 is the first year of the Age of Aquarius.

Shifting eras is always linked with global shocks, crises of civilization, and economic and cultural revolutions, as well as a new perspective on religious teachings. Even the climate usually undergoes major changes.

Summer and autumn 2020, and all of 2021, are clear indicators of that.

The second most important astrological phenomenon is conflict between Saturn and Uranus, which will continue throughout 2021.

Saturn will square Uranus several times in 2021 – we can divide them into the following periods: January-March, May-the first half of July, December 2021-January 2022.

During these periods, we can expect many problems to rear their heads. It is hard to say exactly how this will influence each individual person as part of a general prediction – everything depends on your personal data, though, generally speaking, I can say that we will see the following trends in during these periods of 2021:

I.   First of all, we can expect the economic crisis to expand in scope. Many people will lose their jobs, and companies will go bankrupt.

II. In many countries, we will see social breakdown. People will organize strikes and demonstrations, and the overarching theme will be their discontent with authorities and the current order. We will see confrontation between society and power structures.

III. In global hotspots, we may see new deployments of military force or reescalation of conflict.

IV. For individuals, problems that began in 2019 or 2020 will continue, though this time, things may worsen. Remember – a chain is only as strong as its weakest link.

V.   The climate may undergo significant changes- flooding and forest fires will cause extensive damage. Large-scale migrations will be the result. In response, governments of countries in a better position may declare states of emergency or deploy troops in order to prevent unwanted migrants from crossing their borders.

VI. This interaction between Saturn and Uranus is indicative of conflict between old and new ways of life, and a difficult, irreconcilable struggle that will be reflected in all areas of life – social, economic, and political.

Saturn carries the energy of restrictions and structure. At the same time, Uranus is the planet of unexpected, revolutionary change (as well as high tech). Conflict between the two planets leads to sharp changes in existing reality. Transitioning to a new world and a new set of rules will lead to conflict.

Interaction between Saturn and Uranus speaks to opposition to both new and old ways of living, and of the rigid, irreconcilable struggle that is reflected in every sphere of life – social, economic, and political. Most peoples' lives will undergo dramatic changes, and they will have to adapt.

Economics and Politics

Saturn will square Uranus throughout 2021, and this will raise difficult questions – it is time for out with the old, in with the new. But replacing an old system with a new one is rarely a peaceful process. That is why the struggle between old and new economic orders will be a feature of 2020 and 2021.

Former economic systems will begin to transform, right before our very eyes, and these processes will go hand in hand with trade wars, political reckoning, and in some cases, armed conflict.

As the global financial crisis further unfolds, we can expect to see a stronger China, and weakened United States. Countries in the Western financial system will suffer greatly, particularly those in the Eurozone, and American political and economic satellites.

From an astrological perspective, the American presidential elections will take place during one of the most challenging periods of 2020. By now, we are used to political scandals every four years when they occur. However, I fear that the 2020 elections will put all others to shame when it comes to political upheaval.

On Election Day and the period leading up to it, Mercury and Mars will be in retrograde, which means that there will be significant incorrect or intentionally twisted information, crowds of protesters, and this will peak the last week before the elections take place, on November 3. Retrograde planets also point toward the opposition party trying to protest the election results, which will translate into large-scale scandal.

Donald Trump may be re-elected for a second term, if Joe Biden is his only opponent. Incriminating information on Biden will come to light in late September or October 2020, when he will simultaneously battle serious health issues. Generally speaking, Biden's horoscope is much weaker than Trump's.

Whoever ends up as President of the United States will have to face a series of problems in 2021- most of all conflict among members of his inner circle.

The horoscope of the United States, which was founded on the day of its Declaration of Independence, on July 04, 1776, in Philadelphia, Pennsylvania, USA, predicts that America's economic and political might will waste away, and this may take place more quickly than we can imagine.

This crisis in the American system will lead to a drop and depreciation in the US dollar in late 2020 or the first quarter of 2021. The US chart suggests that in 2021, the dollar will be replaced as a reserve currency.

As America weakens, it will face growing confrontations with other countries. In 2021, the US will wield less influence on political and economic allies.

There may even be tides of separatism within the States themselves.

Even so, I do not think the United States is threatened by the same fate as the USSR – it is unlikely to disintegrate. But it is possible that in late 2020 or early 2021, some states will declare their desire to secede, and even take some decisive steps in that direction, but full secession is not in the cards. Nonetheless, the struggle will be very difficult for America's political elite and society as a whole.

Large-scale social protests and unrest, which we saw in 2019 and 2020 will continue in 2021, though they may become more aggressive in nature.

This does not only apply to the United States. Social activism will grow worldwide. Mottos of the Age of Aquarius are FREEDOM, EQUALITY, and BROTHERHOOD, and they will be brandished in many countries around the world. This time, the conflict will not only be over ethnic or racial issues, but also pit social classes against each other – the rich versus the poor.

During the second half of 2020, and nearly all of 2021, expect an economic crisis that will spare nearly no country around the world. Many will blame their current governments, and brutal confrontations between citizens and the authorities will follow, oppositions will become active, demonstrations will take place, and instability in some countries may go so far as to topple current regimes.

England will also be dragged into financial crisis, and according to its horoscope, the worst period countrywide is likely to begin in December 2020, and last until September 2023. Expect financial problems, changes in the Royal Family (the Queen is likely to leave the throne between December 2020 and July 2021), and also innovative changes to how the country is governed.

There are also indications that in the summer and fall of 2020, a financial crisis is likely in the Russian Federation, and it will continue into 2021.

During this period, President Putin's horoscope contains indications of a systemic crisis, financial shortages, and growing opposition movements. Any leader's horoscope is largely a reflection of the state of his or her country.

Money

All countries will lean more strongly toward virtual currencies and cryptocurrencies, which will be accepted by many countries' governments over the next three to five years. This will make it easier to control cash flow, and with it, all of us.

Our reality will increasingly take place virtually, and professionals in this arena will make up the most sought-after and highly-paid class of workers.

As far as personal finance, the Zodiac sign horoscopes included in my book, "Complete Horoscope 2021" offer more specific information. But generally speaking, during a transition period, it is better to refrain from taking risks, and best to avoid investing your money in get-rich-quick schemes.

What's more, there is a saying "Don't risk your house on a sure thing"- now, that is surprisingly relevant.

Personal life

A crisis is a crisis, but love is an eternal concept. So long as humans exist, they will live and love. 2021 will likely also be a year of major changes in this arena. While tragedy will befall some, others will find happiness.

Unstable partnerships are likely to fall apart, and all the problems faced by unhappy couples are likely to rear their ugly heads.

Unexpected breakups are a possibility, and in many cases, this will be related to an existential crisis, internal discomfort, or maybe even material losses.

Couples with a sincere bond and real affection for one another may be able to take their relationship to the next level, for example, they may begin living together, or get married.

The political, economic, and social shifts underway might force many to move, find a new place to live, or acquire real estate. Many people may also find themselves immersed in issues related to housing- buying or restoring a home, and in some cases, that may be related to moving to another city or even abroad.

In that scenario, be careful and pay attention- due to the conflict between Saturn and Uranus, it is not worth making any investments in a completed construction or second home unless the project has already been proven.

People will begin to seriously reconsider their views on the concept of marriage in the near future. During the Age of Aquarius, bonds between people will be built on ideas of equality and spiritual unity.

The current trend of increasing numbers of non-traditional relationships will only grow stronger.

Differences between the sexes will gradually fade away, as Aquarius is the sign of unisex. Marriage itself will begin to resemble the classic model less and less, as it becomes free, and in some cases, "open". This may bring both advantages and serious disadvantages. Obviously, freedom is a good thing. But that freedom often goes hand in hand with loneliness.

Conflict between Saturn and Uranus will lead to a generational conflict. Saturn represents the older generation, parents, while Uranus represents rebellious children. That means that the younger generation will actively push back against pressure from their elders, and the older generation will need to become wiser and more flexible.

Health

Technology will play a greater role in medicine, affecting every branch of it.

The union of Saturn and Jupiter, and their tension toward Uranus suggest unexpected deaths, which may be due to various types of accidents and cataclysms.

Those suffering from chronic cardiovascular or spinal diseases should take special precautions.

We may encounter a "second wave" of coronavirus, or outbreaks of new, unknown diseases.

I entitled this article "Birth of a New World". Birth is a painful process, and a mother's body undergoes significant changes, but the fact remains that birth is a great joy for parents and loved ones. The same can be said for 2021. It will not be an easy year, and many will have a difficult time – whether they face problems at work or in their personal life, but that is the logical continuation of the period we live in. We will gain experience and knowledge, and see the emergence of new technology, which will open a new chapter in human history. I am certain that after a transition period, the Age of Aquarius will be the beginning of a new, wonderful world.

Tatiana Borsch

July 12, 2020

2021 Overview for Gemini

2021 looks like an obstacle course. On one hand, new opportunities are on the horizon. On the other, new problems are starting to crop up. In any case, there is no way back – there is nowhere to go but forward!

Work. Throughout the year, solar and lunar eclipses will take place both in your sign and your opposite sign. This means everything is in flux, and no area of your life will be left behind.

You will begin seeing new professional opportunities, and in some cases, they will involve moving or developing ties with partners from different cities or abroad. This may mean reconnecting with former associates, but under a new partnership and with a new, more promising foundation.

At the same time, unexpected problems may prevent you from moving full-speed ahead, which will hinder progress somewhat. This may be due to *force majeure*, or possibly, the erratic behavior of colleagues located abroad or in other cities.

Other challenges are likely to stem from a difficult international situation, and are likely to disrupt your plans and work.

Entrepreneurs and management should prepare for audits, which are highly likely during the second half of January, in February, June, and December. During these periods, new legal problems may arise or old ones may rear their heads again.

Things aren't perfect, but despite that, you are steadily moving ahead, and that will start to pay off closer to the end of the year.

Entrepreneurs will break new ground and find a more stable income, while employees can count on new work. Negotiations on this may start as early as Autumn 2021, and things will be in full swing by 2022.

Money. Finances may be uneven in 2021. You still aren't seeing any large income, but your expenses are reasonable and predictable.

Love and family. This year's eclipses will have a major impact on your personal life. This may mean several gripping scenarios.

Single people may meet someone interesting, and love may grow to the point where it's time to start seriously thinking about the future.

After thinking things over, many will be ready to say, "I do" and march straight down the aisle.

Less decisive Geminis might simply move in and begin living together.

However, the eclipses will force many to totally reconsider their current relationships, especially if there have been problems for years. In that case, many spouses and couples will ask themselves, "is it worth staying? Is this the right person for me?" Often, the answer will be "no".

Relationships with family members may become challenging from time to time, and more often than not, this will involve your better half's relatives, rather than your own. This may stem from intrigue, unexpected and damaging information about you, rumors, and gossip. Should this happen, the stars recommend solving the problem calmly, and avoiding conflict whenever possible.

Health. Throughout 2021, your energy levels will remain high enough and you will have no reason to fear getting sick. However, the stars strongly encourage you to be more careful when traveling, and behind the wheel. Critical months in 2021 are the second half of January, February, the second half of May, June, and December. You will find further details in the monthly predictions.

January

This month, you'll need a thoughtful plan, down to the last detail. And keep every possible outcome in mind, without focusing too much on the most pleasant. This way, you'll avoid mistakes, or at least minimize them.

Work. The first half of the month will be calm and predictable. Many will be doing business at home, and that includes methodical, organizational tasks. The second half of the month will be turbulent and chaotic. Several problems will emerge involving associates from other cities or abroad, which will be directly reflected in your working processes. You may have to grapple with an unusual situation, or unpleasant secrets from those around you.

Entrepreneurs and managers at every level may find themselves the target of various auditing authorities, including those from international bodies. If that is your case, keep in mind that things are unlikely to be resolved in January; they will get much more difficult next month.

A planned move or business launch in another city or country will be challenging, and as a result, things will stall or end up on the verge of collapse. In that case, keep a cool head as you deal with the problems, and be patient – time heals all wounds, and this way you will be able to carry out everything you planned and dreamed.

Travel planned for the second half of January may not happen or may turn out to be less-than successful.

Money. January is likely to be neutral, financially speaking. In the first month, expect support from your spouse, parents, or loved ones. During the second half of the month, you can be assured of major expenses, mostly related to solving the problems that will arise.

Love and family. Expect additional difficulties in your personal life this month.

In the first half of January, family life may be calm, but during the second half, you are likely to face problems with family – not your own relatives, but those of your spouse or partner. Perhaps arguments will be likely – family members will face unexpected problems, and you will have to help them, in both word and deed.

Many Geminis will be very busy trying to improve their lives, and this may mean carrying out various repairs, or acquiring items to make everyday life easier or more beautiful.

Health. You are feeling sluggish in January, but not to the point of being seriously ill.

The main danger this month is travel! From January 11 to February 20, be careful and pay attention! Accidents, injuries, and unpleasant incidents behind the wheel are highly likely during this period. Additionally, unless it is absolutely essential, it is better to avoid taking any trips, and that goes for travel for both business or pleasure.

February

You will have some choices to make this month, and they may have major, far-reaching consequences. But you can consider things from all sides, and make the right decision. Stay calm, don't forget the details, and be patient when the wave carries you forward!

Work. You're facing a difficult task at work – take up the fight or leave the game altogether. No one would blame you, if you opted for the latter, but it is unlikely to happen. Closer to the end of the month, you will find your all your work was not in vain.

You might face some obstacles this month that throw a wrench in your plans. They might look differently, depending on your past, and each individual situation.

Those with longstanding ties to colleagues from other cities or countries will tackle various problems that are likely to seriously hamper your path forward.

Alternatively, legal issues loom on the horizon, or perhaps a secret will come to light, either for you or someone in your circle.

These are all things you will have to deal with for all of February, but near the end you will be able to untangle it all and get back on track.

Money. Financially, February looks to be relatively neutral. You are not expected to receive large amounts of money, but your expenses are predictable and within your means.

Love and family. As far as your personal life is concerned, you can expect to run into some problems. Many will have disagreements with family members, and though this is more likely to occur with your in-laws than your own relatives, that is not always the case.

You may discover many things – starting with some unpleasant moments involving your relatives. They might also find out something about you, which will have a negative influence on your relationship.

The stars recommend all Geminis keep a close eye on their words, actions, and avoid any risks to their reputation. That applies to all other areas of life of interest to you, as well.

Health. The main danger you're facing this month is the road. All month long, particularly from the 11th to the 20th of February, be very careful when driving and traveling, whether far away or close to home. Accidents are highly likely, as are other unpleasant incidents.

March

This month will take you right to your edge – but that is not a bad thing. You are on the right track, and the stars are on your side. It seems your time has come!

Work. When it comes to work, March is one of your best months of the year. Your previous problems are nearly resolved, and the path ahead is wide open. Entrepreneurs and managers may conclude favorable transactions and significantly expand their area of activity.

Thanks to your own efforts, difficult relationships from afar will improve a bit. Closer to the end of the month, you are likely to go on a trip, and this time, it looks to be very successful.

Employees may significantly improve their position at work, and may even be promoted. In some cases, this will happen at your current workplace, and in others, somewhere new. Here, everything depends on your plans and intentions. The ball is in your court!

Money. Financial problems are not on the horizon this month. You are making more money, and can expect to receive the largest amounts on March 3, 4, 11, 12, 22, 23, or 30 and 31.

Love and family. March is very work-oriented for you, and you may not have the time or energy for love. But this is not a problem- your loved ones understand, and you will be even closer when things settle down for you at work. Near the end of the month, you will have a chance to go on a trip together, and, even if it is short, you are sure to enjoy yourselves.

Health. Mars is in your sign, which means that you have more than enough energy, and the stars strongly advise you to use it only for peaceful means.

April

Events in April will unfold in such a way that you will have your many talents on full display.

Work. Your greatest achievement this month will be the bright, positive development of connections with colleagues from other cities or abroad. You bring a lot to the table here, and your efforts will be successful.

You may have both allies and assistants right now, but at some point, they might become your friends, or benevolent and high-ranking supporters. By working together, you can move mountains! Though that may not even be necessary – perhaps the mountains will move toward you!

For all work activities, the first half of April is the best period, so try to plan major events during this time.

During the second two weeks of the month, things are also going rather well, though you may face a few problems, which you will fortunately be able to overcome. It is possible that after all this good luck, you will have to examine the details and administrative matters, which is never easy.

Money. Despite your professional success, moneywise, you are stagnating. This is temporary, in all cases. A bit later on, everything you are doing now will translate into a breakthrough, so work on the future, and believe in your star!

Love and family. Something interesting is underway in your personal life. Any moves planned this month may resolve most of your problems, and you will deal with the rest later. You may take a trip or move during the first half of the month, and during the second half, you will get to tackling your everyday problems.

Single people and those who have been let down by love in the past will have a magnificent opportunity to organize their lives. You are highly likely to meet someone who will change your life in April, in some cases that will happen while you are traveling or with people who have come from faraway.

Couples will be able to strengthen their relationship, and get more serious about their future, consider marriage or living together, which is also a good thing.

Health. Most of April, you are feeling energetic, healthy, and charming, which will not go unnoticed. You might start to feel a slight drop in energy around the last ten days of April, so the stars recommend that you slow down a little and pay attention to your body and its needs – rest and sound sleep.

May

A good general always prepares for battle, and that includes the battlefield. That is the task lying before you right now.

Work. The first half of May will not be easy for you, you will have to overcome obstacles which may look differently, depending on each individual case.

You may be dealing with endless questions from associates in other cities or abroad. Or possibly, you will have to tackle complicated administrative matters, which may not always go smoothly. During the second half of the month, however, things will resolve favorably, and work will be moving forward steadily. This month, Jupiter, the lucky planet, is moving into the work-related sector of your sky, which means that you are ahead of the game, and things are going to turn out well for you. Some things may take place a little later than this month, but the most important thing is that they happen!

Money. Your finances are stable, but that's as much as you can say. You will not see any windfall this month, but your expenses are reasonable and within your means. You may get some small income from unofficial sources. In many cases, it will take the form of support from loved ones.

Love and family. The first half of the month is more suitable for personal, family matters, and many Geminis are busy with just that. You might relax with some family members, but it's best to avoid any travel this month – things may not turn out as you hoped and dreamed.

During the second half of the month, however, you have an excellent opportunity to travel, whether for business or pleasure.

This is a wonderful time to meet new people, and to deepen existing relationships, too.

The May eclipse promises a new romance with lasting consequences. For single people, this may be an escape from many problems. But if you are already in a relationship, buckle up – the flames of passion may burn a lot hotter than you originally intended.

Health. During the first half of May, you are feeling sluggish, so take care of yourself and remain vigilant. Exercise particular caution when traveling or driving. There is a very high probability of unfortunate incidents and accidents during this period. During the second half of the month, things look brighter – you will feel more energetic and things will feel easier.

June

You're on full alert as you celebrate your birthday. That's not a bad thing, as positive changes are on the horizon, but first, you'll have to fight for them!

Work. This month, your ruler, Mercury, is in retrograde, so many of the things you have to work on are suddenly going much more slowly than expected. This is happening to all Geminis, regardless of their field.

Employees are planning on transferring to a new job, and that might involve somewhere faraway, moving, or active cooperation with associates in other cities or abroad. The possibilities of this development are encouraging, but during the middle of June, you will suddenly come up against obstacles that will throw a wrench in your plans. They may be laws from another country, unexpected, negative information sullying your reputation, or perhaps even force majeure.

Entrepreneurs planning to launch in a new country or cooperate with associates from out of town may run into similar problems. But thanks to your heroic efforts, most things will smooth over, and you will be able to deal with the rest, later.

Money. Your finances are up and down. Money will be coming in regularly, but your expenses are expected to increase. At the end of the month, however, you will see a positive balance, perhaps because of a large sum that will be coming in in both mid- and late June.

Love and family. In your personal life, you might face a whole range of problems. Your relationship with relatives has grown complicated – during the middle and end of June, you can expect serious arguments, which will drag your entire family into the fray.

During this period, some information will come to light, which will have a negative impact on your relationships, and force you to reconsider many of them. Alternatively, a relative might face serious problems and you will have to help them, in either words or deeds.

June will also be a challenging month for couples. They might find that it is difficult to see each other as much as they would like, or perhaps they will have trouble reaching an understanding.

Those who are moving somewhere faraway will face challenges to overcome in both June and July.

Health. This month, you might experience anxiety, stress, and an emotional rollercoaster, which will be reflected in your mood and well-being.

Try to get enough sleep, and remember that excessive anxiety is not healthy.

And remember to be extra cautious when traveling and driving, especially in mid- to late June!

July

This month, the stars' positive and negative influences will seemingly engage in a fanciful pas-de-deux, and you will need to be flexible as you maneuver between them, in order to leverage the former, and avoid the latter.

Work. During the first ten days of July, you can expect to feel tense. Problems that were making your life difficult in the past will continue during this time.

Many Geminis will once again have to deal with inconsistencies from colleagues from other cities or abroad, which, in many cases, will once again drive many negotiations close to the point of breaking down. Can things turn around? Yes, and you will be the one to do it. Your efforts will drive necessary changes, and contribute to getting relationships back on the right track.

There are also positive trends afoot. From July 11 to 31, you may receive tempting business offers, whether you are an employee or entrepreneur.

For now, things are still in the negotiation phase, but they will certainly lead to success in the near future.

Money. Your finances are clearly improving, and you can expect to receive the largest sums on July 9, 10, 18, 19, 26, and 27.

Love and family. During the first ten days of July, prepare to deal with problems in your family life, too. During this period, a difficult situation from the past will continue involving your relatives.

This time, however, the issues may take an unexpected and very unpleasant turn. You will need to be flexible as you maneuver between two feuding family members, or resolve relatives' difficult problems.

This month, and especially during the first ten days of July, expect certain secrets to suddenly be brought to light – they may be yours or those of someone you know. This will complicate relationships, including for couples or spouses, if they have anything to hide from each other. Remember this, and keep a close eye on developments.

Things will calm down during the rest of the month. This is a good time for traveling, resolving problems that have appeared, and working on your troubled relationships.

Single people will have an excellent opportunity to meet someone interesting, and, most likely, that will take place while you are traveling, or among people who have come from afar.

Health. This month, you are feeling energized and are not at risk of falling ill. During the first ten days of July, however, be very careful while traveling or driving. There is a high likelihood of accidents and injuries during this time!

August

The changes are continuing. In order to grow a new garden, you need to clean out the flower beds and weed. And that is exactly what you are going to need to do right now.

Work. During the first ten days of August, many Geminis can expect to face a series of problems. In some cases, it may revolve around overcoming legal issues, or possibly, involve colleagues from afar. In other cases, you will have to deal with another country's laws, over the course of the entire month.

During the second half of August, your main task might be conducting various transactions involving real estate or other property, which is particularly relevant to those planning a move or a business launch in another city or abroad.

Employees might carry out negotiations with counterparts from another city or abroad, but they will also have to overcome several obstacles, which will stall everything for a while. Things will even out by December 2021, but in the meantime, keep following your plans, and stay the course – don't even take one step away from it – you'll achieve everything you want!

Money. Financially speaking, this month is likely to be neutral. You have some expenses, but your income is also modest, and most of it is not from your normal workplace.

You can expect money from various real estate transactions, or assistance from parents or loved one.

Love and family. Your personal life will be full of unpleasant surprises during the first half of August. Once again, this will involve your relatives, and, in some cases, longstanding feuds, and in others, problems with close family members.

Those in the middle of long-distance moves will have to resolve various matters near the end of the month, and they will be related to your home. This will continue into September, too.

In all cases, you will be able to count on loved ones for support, both at home and at work. They may be your parents, spouse, or older relative. That help will be most noticeable during the second half of August, when many Geminis will have to outfit a new home. It is very possible that this will take place in another city or country.

Health. Your energy is running high in August, and you are not at risk of falling ill. Nonetheless, the stars strongly urge you to be careful when traveling and driving. The first ten days of the month will be the most dangerous.

September

"There's no place like home" and "my home is my castle" are your mottos in September.

Work. September is a time for putting your finances in order and getting organized. This is what entrepreneurs and managers are doing, if they plan to open their own business, and in some cases, that will be in another city or abroad.

Various problems and stressors from the past seem to be resolved, now, and you can now dedicate all of your efforts to the work at hand, which bodes well for the future.

You will reconnect with long-term associates from other cities or abroad, and you might have productive meetings or favorable negotiations, too.

Employees will take a short trip somewhere and focus on family or home, which is especially relevant if you are moving somewhere new.

All changes at work are clearly for the better. You are beginning a new chapter, and it promises to be a successful one!

Money. Your financial situation is stable, but most of your money will come from such as sponsorship, credit, and support from parents or a loved one. You may also receive profits from various real estate transactions, whether from sales or rent.

Love and family. Many Geminis will find that September is a time for getting their personal affairs in order. You are likely to change your living space – repairing or buying an apartment, home, or perhaps something else related to home improvement.

In all cases, this month you are likely to see strong influence from your parents and elder family members, especially your mother. In addition to moral support, you might count on material help as well.

Parents will focus on their children's future, and might spend a lot of time on their development and education. You are likely to see some problems in this area toward the end of the month, and in October, as well.

September is a good month for couples, as well. After sleepless nights and worries, they might decide to live together, and in some cases, to get married.

The first half of September is the best time for both personal and professional events.

The last ten days of September will be less dynamic, as your ruler, Mercury, will move into retrograde after September 27. That means that you can expect setbacks at work, and various problems. This period will continue until October 18, so it is worth tackling any important tasks during the first 20 days of the month.

Health. In September, you are feeling somewhat sluggish, but if you watch your schedule, you will be able to avoid any problems You might find yourself gaining weight, so don't forget to exercise and watch your diet.

October

It's time to pay attention to what is happening around you. Be sensitive to your partner, and you will be pleasantly surprised with the results.

Work. Even if many Geminis see big changes in their personal and romantic lives this month, incorrigible workaholics will still be able to achieve a lot at work.

You can improve your relationship with colleagues in other cities or abroad, work on legal issues, and also get any necessary paperwork in order.

This is how the first twenty days of October will play out. During the last ten days, things will become more dynamic, as well as challenging. You will have to grapple with difficult issues related to promoting new projects or holding delicate negotiations for a new job.

Many Geminis will be able to overcome these challenges related to opening a new business somewhere far away, or perhaps legal issues, the laws in another country, or partners' reticence to meeting you halfway.

Money. Expect financial instability in October. During the first twenty days of the month, you will have expenses related to your children, loved ones, or home improvement.

You can count on some money on October 1, 16, 17, 26, and 27.

Love and family. Many events will be related to your personal life in October. Parents will spend time with their children, who will require your attention and care. It's possible that their needs will also involve a large part of your family's budget.

Couples might see their dreams come true, and this may involve marriage. Much of October will be devoted to this major issue.

It seems that everything is going well, but at some point, you will begin to have doubts again. It is not worth sharing these thoughts with your partner, as any doubts and hesitation are your problem, not theirs. Work on these matters on your own, before acting.

Those who are moving somewhere far away will have to deal with issues related to setting up their home, their children's future, and will find themselves very busy with these bothersome tasks.

Health. This month, you are healthy and energetic, but also stressed and anxious. In this case, be sure to get enough sleep, and get regular meals.

November

You have been moving ahead at a steady pace, but this month, you are unlikely to see much progress. The road ahead is winding, but you will manage everything!

Work. This month, those in the business world will once again face challenges. It might be that you have overcome a lot of obstacles in the past, but right now, you will have to take a step back and re-examine some annoying issues.

In some cases, an established relationship with colleagues in other cities or abroad may now need some attention and adjustments. Alternatively, you will have to go back to some legal issues, which have suddenly taken an unexpected twist.

On top of all that, you may run into unexpected audits, which will put a damper on some of your plans, but will not stall them entirely.

Employees should be careful with colleagues, as there is intrigue and other unhealthy dynamics brewing on your team.

Managers and entrepreneurs should be cautious when dealing with subordinates – someone might interfere with your plans, intentionally or not.

All relationships will become more difficult during the first twenty days of the month, and only get back on track during the last ten days of November. It seems that, once again, you are overcoming problems and finding your way, with minimal losses.

Money. Financially, November will be up and down. You will not end up penniless, but your expenses will be rather high. A lot of them may be related to your problems at work.

Love and family. Your personal life may occupy less of your time this month, compared to things at work. If you spend most of your time at home with your family or romantic partner, however, you can count on November bringing some secrets to light, which will complicate your relationship with those around you.

This goes for married and unmarried couples, so buckle up, especially if there are things you would prefer remained in the dark.

You might also experience problems with relatives, either your own or those of your partner. In that case, you can expect that your own secrets will be revealed, as well as those of your loved ones.

This will make relationships much more difficult, but things will stop short of outright catastrophe. Maybe both sides will think about things, talk it over, and manage to forgive and understand each other.

Health. The first twenty days of November will be challenging for your health. You might feel very weak, and see chronic conditions exacerbate.

Additionally, the stars strongly recommend being very careful while traveling, driving, or using electric appliances. There is a strong likelihood of injury or accident this month.

December

The stars are urging you to help others, but don't forget about yourself. If you able to combine these two opposing trends, you are sure to win.

Work. Your business partners will exert powerful influence all month long. With their assistance, you will be able to resolve difficult relationships with colleagues in other cities or abroad, and reach the next level, professionally.

2021 has not been an easy year for you, but things are about to improve – you will feel calmer, and the road to success is opening right now.

December will not be easy, either, and you can expect various situations to become more difficult at both the beginning and end of the month. You may have to grapple with challenging relationships with colleagues from other cities or abroad, or possibly, you will have to deal with old legal problems, instead. In the end, though, everything will resolve in your favor, and closer to the end of the month, you will be able to celebrate your victory.

Money. Financially, you are also fighting an uphill battle. You will be spending constantly, and in some cases, that will stem from resolving issues at work, while in others, your home and family will be the source. During the worst periods, a business partner, spouse, parents, or other loved one may help you.

Love and family. Many Geminis will be busy with their personal life, and to a certain extent, follow the lead of a loved one. You will not have to wait long for a response. In return, you might receive support – either moral or financial – if you need it. If the issue concerns your relatives, which is very likely at the beginning or end of December, your partner might play a major role in resolving matters.

Many Geminis will have an encounter with a former partner who now lives in another city or abroad.

Those who are moving somewhere far away this month might have to resolve major domestic quandaries, such as how to set up a home somewhere new.

Health. You are not particularly energetic this month, and that is most noticeable as December comes to a close. During this time, remember to take care of yourself, take some time to relax, and get enough sleep.

A guide to Zodiac compatibility

Often, when we meet a person, we get a feeling that they are good and we take an instant liking to them. Another person, however, gives us immediate feelings of distrust, fear and hostility. Is there an astrological reason why people say that 'the first impression is the most accurate'? How can we detect those who will bring us nothing but trouble and unhappiness?

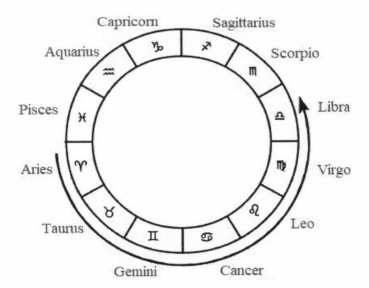

Without going too deeply into astrological subtleties unfamiliar to some readers, it is possible to determine the traits according to which friendship, love or business relationships will develop.

Let's begin with problematic relationships - our most difficult are with our **8th sign**. For example, for Aries the 8th sign is Scorpio, for Taurus it is Sagittarius and so on. Finding your 8th sign is easy; assume your own sign to be first (see above Figure) and then move eight signs counter clockwise around the Zodiac circle. This is also how the other signs (fourth, ninth and so on) that we mention are to be found.

Ancient astrologers variously referred to the 8th sign as the symbol of death, of destruction, of fated love or unfathomable attraction. In astrological terms, this pair is called 'master and slave' or 'boa constrictor and rabbit', with the role of 'master' or 'boa constrictor' being played by our 8th sign.

This relationship is especially difficult for politicians and business people.

We can take the example of a recent political confrontation in the USA. Hilary Clinton is a Scorpio while Donald Trump is a Gemini - her 8th sign. Even though many were certain that Clinton would be elected President, she lost.

To take another example, Hitler was a Taurus and his opponents – Stalin and Churchill - were both of his 8th sign, Sagittarius. The result of their confrontation is well known. Interestingly, the Russian Marshals who dealt crushing military blows to Hitler and so helped end the Third Reich - Konstantin Rokossovsky and Georgy Zhukov - were also Sagittarian, Hitler's 8th sign.

In another historical illustration, Lenin was also a Taurus. Stalin was of Lenin's 8th sign and was ultimately responsible for the downfall and possibly death of his one-time comrade-in-arms.

Business ties with those of our 8th sign are hazardous as they ultimately lead to stress and loss; both financial and moral. So, do not tangle with your 8th sign and never fight with it - your chances of winning are remote!

Such relationships are very interesting in terms of love and romance, however. We are magnetically attracted to our 8th sign and even though it may be very intense physically, it is very difficult for family life; 'Feeling bad when together, feeling worse when apart'.

As an example, let us take the famous lovers - George Sand who was Cancer and Alfred de Musset who was Sagittarius. Cancer is the 8th sign for Sagittarius, and the story of their crazy two-year love affair was the subject of much attention throughout France. Critics and writers were divided into 'Mussulist' and 'Sandist' camps; they debated fiercely about who was to blame for the sad ending to their love story - him or her. It's hard to imagine the energy needed to captivate the public for so long, but that energy was destructive for the couple. Passion raged in their hearts, but neither of them was able to comprehend their situation.

Georges Sand wrote to Musset, "*I ·on't love you anymore, an· I will always a·ore you. I ·on't want you anymore, an· I can't ·o without you. It seems that nothing but a heavenly lightning strike can heal me by ·estroying me. Goo·-bye! Stay or go, but ·on't say that I am not suffering. This is the only thing that can make me suffer even more, my love, my life, my bloo·! Go away, but kill me, leaving.*" Musset replied only in brief, but its power surpassed Sand's tirade, "*When you embrace· me, I felt something that is still bothering me, making it impossible for me to approach another woman.*" These two people loved each other passionately and for two years lived together in a powder keg of passion, hatred and treachery.

When someone enters into a romantic liaison with their 8th sign, there will be no peace; indeed, these relationships are very attractive to those who enjoy the edgy, the borderline and, in the Dostoevsky style, the melodramatic. The first to lose interest in the relationship is, as a rule, the 8th sign.

If, by turn of fate, our child is born under our 8th sign, they will be very different from us and, in some ways, not live up to our expectations. It may be best to let them choose their own path.

In business and political relationships, the combination with our **12th sign** is also a complicated one.

We can take two political examples. Angela Merkel is a Cancer while Donald Trump is a Gemini - her 12th sign. This is why their relations are strained and complicated and we can even perhaps assume that the American president will achieve his political goals at her expense. Boris

Yeltsin (Aquarius) was the 12th sign to Mikhail Gorbachev (Pisces) and it was Yeltsin who managed to dethrone the champion of Perestroika.

Even ancient astrologers noticed that our relationships with our 12th signs can never develop evenly; it is one of the most curious and problematic combinations. They are our hidden enemies and they seem to be digging a hole for us; they ingratiate themselves with us, discover our innermost secrets. As a result, we become bewildered and make mistakes when we deal with them. Among the Roman emperors murdered by members of their entourage, there was an interesting pattern - all the murderers were the 12th sign of the murdered.

We can also see this pernicious effect in Russian history: the German princess Alexandra (Gemini) married the last Russian Tsar Nicholas II (Taurus) - he was her 12th sign and brought her a tragic death. The wicked genius Grigory Rasputin (Cancer) made friends with Tsarina Alexandra, who was his 12th sign, and was murdered as a result of their odd friendship. The weakness of Nicholas II was exposed, and his authority reduced after the death of the economic and social reformer Pyotr Stolypin, who was his 12th sign. Thus, we see a chain of people whose downfall was brought about by their 12th sign.

So, it makes sense to be cautious of your 12th sign, especially if you have business ties. Usually, these people know much more about us than we want them to and they will often reveal our secrets for personal gain if it suits them. However, the outset of these relationships is, as a rule, quite normal - sometimes the two people will be friends, but sooner or later one will betray the other one or divulge a secret; inadvertently or not.

In terms of romantic relationships, our 12th sign is gentle, they take care of us and are tender towards us. They know our weaknesses well but accept them with understanding. It is they who guide us, although sometimes almost imperceptibly. Sexual attraction is usually strong.

For example, Meghan Markle is a Leo, the 12th sign for Prince Harry, who is a Virgo. Despite Queen Elizabeth II being lukewarm about the match, Harry's love was so strong that they did marry.

If a child is our 12th sign, it later becomes clear that they know all our secrets, even those that they are not supposed to know. It is very difficult to control them as they do everything in their own way.

Relations with our 7th **sign** are also interesting. They are like our opposite; they have something to learn from us while we, in turn, have something to learn from them. This combination, in business and personal relationships, can be very positive and stimulating provided that both partners are quite intelligent and have high moral standards but if not, constant misunderstandings and challenges follow. Marriage or co-operation with the 7th sign can only exist as the union of two fully-fledged individuals and in this case love, significant business achievements and social success are possible.

However, the combination can be not only interesting, but also quite complicated.

An example is Angelina Jolie, a Gemini, and Brad Pitt, a Sagittarius. This is a typical bond with a 7th sign - it's lively and interesting, but rather stressful. Although such a couple may quarrel and even part from time to time, never do they lose interest in each other.

This may be why this combination is more stable in middle-age when there is an understanding of the true nature of marriage and partnership. In global, political terms, this suggests a state of eternal tension - a cold war - for example between Yeltsin (Aquarius) and Bill Clinton (Leo).

Relations with our 9th **sign** are very good; they are our teacher and advisor - one who reveals things we are unaware of and our relationships with them very often involve travel or re-location. The combination can lead to spiritual growth and can be beneficial in terms of business.

Although, for example, Trump and Putin are political opponents, they can come to an understanding and even feel a certain sympathy for each other because Putin is a Libra while Trump is a Gemini, his 9th sign.

This union is also quite harmonious for conjugal and romantic relationships.

We treat our **3ʳᵈ sign** somewhat condescendingly. They are like our younger siblings; we teach them and expect them to listen attentively. Our younger brothers and sisters are more often than not born under this sign. In terms of personal and sexual relationships, the union is not very inspiring and can end quickly, although this is not always the case. In terms of business, it is fairly average as it often connects partners from different cities or countries.

We treat our **5ᵗʰ sign** as a child and we must take care of them accordingly. The combination is not very good for business, however, since our 5ᵗʰ sign triumphs over us in terms of connections and finances, and thereby gives us very little in return save for love or sympathy. However, they are very good for family and romantic relationships, especially if the 5ᵗʰ sign is female. If a child is born as a 5ᵗʰ sign to their parents, their relationship will be a mutually smooth, loving and understanding one that lasts a lifetime.

Our **10ᵗʰ sign** is a born leader. Depending on the spiritual level of those involved, both pleasant and tense relations are possible; the relationship is often mutually beneficial in the good times but mutually disruptive in the bad times. In family relations, our 10ᵗʰ sign always tries to lead and will do so according to their intelligence and upbringing.

Our **4ᵗʰ sign** protects our home and can act as a sponsor to strengthen our financial or moral positions. Their advice should be heeded in all cases as it can be very effective, albeit very unobtrusive. If a woman takes this role, the relationship can be long and romantic, since all the spouse's wishes are usually met one way or another. Sometimes, such couples achieve great social success; for instance, Hilary Clinton, a Scorpio is the 4ᵗʰ sign to Bill Clinton, a Leo. On the other hand, if the husband is the 4ᵗʰ sign for his wife, he tends to be henpecked. There is often a strong sexual attraction. Our 4ᵗʰ sign can improve our living conditions and care for us in a parental way. If a child is our 4ᵗʰ sign, they are close to us and support us affectionately.

Relations with our **11ᵗʰ sign** are often either friendly or patronizing; we treat them reverently, while they treat us with friendly condescension. Sometimes, these relationships develop in an 'older brother' or 'high-ranking friend' sense; indeed, older brothers and sisters are often our 11th sign. In terms of personal and sexual relationships, our 11th sign is always inclined to enslave us. This tendency is most clearly manifested in such alliances as Capricorn and Pisces or Leo and Libra. A child who is the 11th sign to their parents will achieve greater success than their parents, but this will only make the parents proud.

Our **2nd sign** should bring us financial or other benefits; we receive a lot from them in both our business and our family life. In married couples, the 2nd sign usually looks after the financial situation for the benefit of the family. Sexual attraction is strong.

Our **6th sign** is our 'slave'; we always benefit from working with them and it's very difficult for them to escape our influence. In the event of hostility, especially if they have provoked the conflict, they receive a powerful retaliatory strike. In personal relations, we can almost destroy them by making them dance to our tune. For example, if a husband doesn't allow his wife to work or there are other adverse family circumstances, she gradually becomes lost as an individual despite being surrounded by care. This is the best-case scenario; worse outcomes are possible. Our 6th sign has a strong sexual attraction to us because we are the fatal 8th sign for them; we cool down quickly, however, and often make all kinds of demands. If the relationship with our 6th sign is a long one, there is a danger that routine, boredom and stagnation will ultimately destroy the relationship. A child born under our 6th sign needs particularly careful handling as they can feel fear or embarrassment when communicating with us. Their health often needs increased attention and we should also remember that they are very different from us emotionally.

Finally, we turn to relations with **our own sign**. Scorpio with Scorpio and Cancer with Cancer get along well, but in most other cases, however, our own sign is of little interest to us as it has a similar energy. Sometimes, this relationship can develop as a rivalry, either in business or in love.

There is another interesting detail - we are often attracted to one particular sign. For example, a man's wife and mistress often have the same sign. If there is confrontation between the two, the stronger character displaces the weaker one. As an example, Prince Charles is a Scorpio, while both Princess Diana and Camilla Parker Bowles were born under the sign of Cancer. Camilla was the more assertive and became dominant.

Of course, in order to draw any definitive conclusions, we need an individually prepared horoscope, but the above always, one way or another, manifests itself.

Love description of Zodiac Signs

We know that human sexual behavior has been studied at length. Entire libraries have been written about it, with the aim of helping us understand ourselves and our partners. But is that even possible? It may not be; no matter how smart we are, when it comes to love and sex, there is always an infinite amount to learn. But we have to strive for perfection, and astrology, with its millennia of research, twelve astrological types, and twelve zodiac signs, may hold the key. Below, you will find a brief and accurate description of each zodiac sign's characteristics in love, for both men and women.

Men

ARIES

Aries men are not particularly deep or wise, but they make up for it in sincerity and loyalty. They are active, even aggressive lovers, but a hopeless romantic may be lurking just below the surface. Aries are often monogamous and chivalrous men, for whom there is only one woman (of course, in her absence, they can sleep around with no remorse). If the object of your affection is an Aries, be sure to give him a lot of sex, and remember that for an Aries, when it comes to sex, anything goes. Aries cannot stand women who are negative or disheveled. They need someone energetic, lively, and to feel exciting feelings of romance.

The best partner for an Aries is Cancer, Sagittarius, or Leo. Aquarius can also be a good match, but the relationship will be rather friendly in nature. Partnering with a Scorpio or Taurus will be difficult, but they can be stimulating lovers for an Aries. Virgos are good business contacts, but a poor match as lovers or spouses.

TAURUS

A typical Taurean man is warm, friendly, gentle, and passionate, even if he doesn't always show it. He is utterly captivated by the beauty of the female body, and can find inspiration in any woman. A Taurus has such excess physical and sexual prowess, that to him, sex is a way to relax and calm down. He is the most passionate and emotional lover of the Zodiac, but he expects his partner to take the initiative, and if she doesn't, he will easily find someone else. Taureans rarely divorce, and are true to the end – if not sexually, at least spiritually. They are secretive, keep their cards close, and may have secret lovers. If a Taurus does not feel a deep emotional connection with someone, he won't be shy to ask her friends for their number. He prefers a voluptuous figure over an athletic or skinny woman.

The best partners for a Taurus are Cancer, Virgo, Pisces, or Scorpio. Sagittarius can show a Taurus real delights in both body and spirit, but they are unlikely to make it down the aisle. They can have an interesting relationship with an Aquarius – these signs are very different, but sometimes can spend their lives together. They might initially feel attracted to an Aries, before rejecting her.

GEMINI

The typical Gemini man is easygoing and polite. He is calm, collected, and analytical. For a Gemini, passion is closely linked to intellect, to the point that they will try to find an explanation for their actions before carrying them out. But passion cannot be explained, which scares a Gemini, and they begin jumping from one extreme to the other. This is why you will find more bigamists among Geminis than any other sign of the Zodiac. Sometimes, Gemini men even have two families, or divorce and marry several times throughout the course of their lives. This may be because they simply can't let new and interesting experiences pass them by. A Gemini's wife or lover needs to be smart, quick, and always looking ahead. If she isn't, he will find a new object for his affection.

Aquarians, Libras, and Aries make good partners for a Gemini. A Sagittarius can be fascinating for him, but they will not marry before he reaches middle age, as both partners will be fickle while they are younger. A Gemini and Scorpio are likely to be a difficult match, and the Gemini will try to wriggle out of the Scorpio's tight embrace. A Taurus will be an exciting sex partner, but their partnership won't be for long, and the Taurus is often at fault.

CANCER

Cancers tend to be deep, emotional individuals, who are both sensitive and highly sexual. Their charm is almost mystical, and they know how to use it. Cancers may be the most promiscuous sign of the Zodiac, and open to absolutely anything in bed. Younger Cancers look for women who are more mature, as they are skilled lovers. As they age, they look for someone young enough to be their own daughter, and delight in taking on the role of a teacher. Cancers are devoted to building a family and an inviting home, but once they achieve that goal, they are likely to have a wandering eye. They will not seek moral justification, as they sincerely believe it is simply something everyone does. Their charm works in such a way that women are deeply convinced they are the most important love in a Cancer's life, and that circumstances are the only thing preventing them from being together. Remember that a Cancer man is a master manipulator, and will not be yours unless he is sure you have throngs of admirers. He loves feminine curves, and is turned on by exquisite fragrances. Cancers don't end things with old lovers, and often go back for a visit after a breakup. Another type of Cancer is rarer – a faithful friend, and up for anything in order to provide for his wife and children. He is patriotic and a responsible worker.

Scorpios, Pisces, and other Cancers are a good match. A Taurus can make for a lasting relationship, as both signs place great value on family and are able to get along with one another. A Sagittarius will result in fights and blowouts from the very beginning, followed by conflicts and breakups. The Sagittarius will suffer the most. Marriage to an Aries isn't off the table, but it won't last very long.

LEO

A typical Leo is handsome, proud, and vain, with a need to be the center of attention at all times. They often pretend to be virtuous, until they are able to actually master it. They crave flattery, and prefer women who comply and cater to them. Leos demand unconditional obedience, and constant approval. When a Leo is in love, he is fairly sexual, and capable of being devoted and faithful. Cheap love affairs are not his thing, and Leos are highly aware of how expensive it is to divorce. They make excellent fathers. A Leo's partner needs to look polished and well-dressed, and he will not tolerate either frumpiness or nerds.

Aries, Sagittarius, and Gemini make for good matches. Leos are often very beguiling to Libras; this is the most infamous astrological "master-slave" pairing. Leos are also inexplicably drawn to Pisces – this is the only sign capable of taming them. A Leo and Virgo will face a host of problems sooner or later, and they might be material in nature. The Virgo will attempt to conquer him, and if she does, a breakup is inevitable.

VIRGO

Virgo is a highly intellectual sign, who likes to take a step back and spend his time studying the big picture. But love inherently does not lend itself to analysis, and this can leave Virgos feeling perplexed. While Virgo is taking his time, studying the object of his affection, someone else will swoop in and take her away, leaving him bitterly disappointed. Perhaps for that reason, Virgos tend to marry late, but once they are married, they remain true, and hardly ever initiate divorce. In bed, they are modest and reserved, as they see sex as some sort of quirk of nature, designed solely for procreation. Most Virgos have a gifted sense of taste, hearing, and smell. They cannot tolerate pungent odors and can be squeamish; they believe their partners should always take pains to be very clean. Virgos usually hate over-the-top expressions of love, and are immune to sex as a mean s of control. Many Virgos are stingy and more appropriate as husbands than lovers. Male Virgos tend to be monogamous, though if they are unhappy or disappointed with their partner, they may begin to look for comfort elsewhere and often give in to drunkenness.

Taurus, Capricorn, and Scorpio make the best partners for a Virgo. They may feel inexplicable attraction for Aquarians. They will form friendships with Aries, but rarely will this couple make it down the aisle. With Leos, be careful – this sign is best as a lover, not a spouse.

LIBRA

Libra is a very complex, wishy-washy sign. They are constantly seeking perfection, which often leaves them in discord with the reality around them. Libra men are elegant and refined, and expect no less from their partner. Many Libras treat their partners like a beautiful work of art, and have trouble holding onto the object of their affection. They view love itself as a very abstract concept, and can get tired of the physical aspect of their relationship. They are much more drawn to intrigue and the chase- dreams, candlelit evenings, and other symbols of romance. A high percentage of Libra men are gay, and they view sex with other men as the more elite option. Even when Libras are unhappy in their marriages, they never divorce willingly. Their wives might leave them, however, or they might be taken away by a more decisive partner.

Aquarius and Gemini make the best matches for Libras. Libra can also easily control an independent Sagittarius, and can easily fall under the influence of a powerful and determined Leo, before putting all his strength and effort into breaking free. Relationships with Scorpios are difficult; they may become lovers, but will rarely marry.

SCORPIO

Though it is common to perceive Scorpios as incredibly sexual, they are, in fact, very unassuming, and never brag about their exploits. They will, however, be faithful and devoted to the right woman. The Scorpio man is taciturn, and you can't expect any tender words from him, but he will defend those he loves to the very end. Despite his outward control, Scorpio is very emotional; he needs and craves love, and is willing to fight for it. Scorpios are incredible lovers, and rather than leaving them tired, sex leaves them feeling energized. They are always sexy, even if they aren't particularly handsome. They are unconcerned with the ceremony of wooing you, and more focused on the act of love itself.

Expressive Cancers and gentle, amenable Pisces make the best partners. A Scorpio might also fall under the spell of a Virgo, who is adept at taking the lead. Sparks might fly between two Scorpios, or with a Taurus, who is perfect for a Scorpio in bed. Relationships with Libras, Sagittarians, and Aries are difficult.

SAGITTARIUS

Sagittarian men are lucky, curious, and gregarious. Younger Sagittarians are romantic, passionate, and burning with desire to experience every type of love. Sagittarius is a very idealistic sign, and in that search for perfection, they tend to flit from one partner to another, eventually forgetting what they were even looking for in the first place. A negative Sagittarius might have two or three relationships going on at once, assigning each partner a different day of the week. On the other hand, a positive Sagittarius will channel his powerful sexual energy into creativity, and take his career to new heights. Generally speaking, after multiple relationships and divorces, the Sagittarian man will conclude that his ideal marriage is one where his partner is willing to look the other way.

Aries and Leo make the best matches for a Sagittarius. He might fall under the spell of a Cancer, but would not be happy being married to her. Gemini can be very intriguing, but will only make for a happy marriage after middle age, when both partners are older and wiser. Younger Sagittarians often marry Aquarian women, but things quickly fall apart. Scorpios can make for an interesting relationship, but if the Sagittarius fails to comply, divorce is inevitable.

CAPRICORN

Practical, reserved Capricorn is one of the least sexual signs of the Zodiac. He views sex as an idle way to pass the time, and something he can live without, until he wants to start a family. He tends to marry late, and almost never divorces. Young Capricorns are prone to suppressing their sexual desires, and only discover them later in life, when they have already achieved everything a real man needs – a career and money. We'll be frank – Capricorn is not the best lover, but he can compensate by being caring, attentive, and showering you with valuable gifts. Ever cautious, Capricorn loves to schedule his sexual relationships, and this is something partners will just have to accept. Women should understand that Capricorn needs some help relaxing – perhaps with alcohol. They prefer inconspicuous, unassuming women, and run away from a fashion plate.

The best partners for a Capricorn are Virgo, Taurus, or Scorpio. Cancers might catch his attention, and if they marry, it is likely to be for life. Capricorn is able to easily dominate Pisces, and Pisces-Capricorn is a well-known "slave and master" combination. Relationships with Leos tend to be erratic, and they are unlikely to wed. Aries might make for a cozy family at first, but things will cool off quickly, and often, the marriage only lasts as long as Capricorn is unwilling to make a change in his life.

AQUARIUS

Aquarian men are mercurial, and often come off as peculiar, unusual, or aloof, and detached. Aquarians are turned on by anything novel or strange, and they are constantly looking for new and interesting people. They are stimulated by having a variety of sexual partners, but they consider this to simply be normal life, rather than sexually immoral. Aquarians are unique – they are more abstract than realistic, and can be cold and incomprehensible, even in close relationships. Once an Aquarius gets married, he will try to remain within the realm of decency, but often fails. An Aquarian's partners need uncommon patience, as nothing they do can restrain him. Occasionally, one might encounter another kind of Aquarius – a responsible, hard worker, and exemplary family man.

The best matches for an Aquarius are female fellow Aquarians, Libras, and Sagittarians. When Aquarius seeks out yet another affair, he is not choosy, and will be happy with anyone.

PISCES

Pisces is the most eccentric sign of the Zodiac. This is reflected in his romantic tendencies and sex life. Pisces men become very dependent on those with whom they have a close relationship. Paradoxically, they are simultaneously crafty and childlike when it comes to playing games, and they are easily deceived. As a double bodied sign, Pisces rarely marry just once, as they are very sexual, easily fall in love, and are constantly seeking their ideal. Pisces are very warm people, who love to take care of others and are inclined toward "slave-master" relationships, in which they are the submissive partner. But after catering to so many lovers, Pisces will remain elusive. They are impossible to figure out ahead of time – today, they might be declaring their love for you, but tomorrow, they may disappear – possibly forever! To a Pisces, love is a fantasy, illusion, and dream, and they might spend their whole lives in pursuit of it. Pisces who are unhappy in love are vulnerable to alcoholism or drug addiction.

Cancer and Scorpio make the best partners for a Pisces. He is also easily dominated by Capricorn and Libra, but in turn will conquer even a queen-like Leo. Often, they are fascinated by Geminis – if they marry, it will last a long time, but likely not forever. Relationships with Aries and Sagittarians are erratic, though initially, things can seem almost perfect.

Women

ARIES

Aries women are leaders. They are decisive, bold, and very protective. An Aries can take initiative and is not afraid to make the first move. Her ideal man is strong, and someone she can admire. But remember, at the slightest whiff of weakness, she will knock him off his pedestal. She does not like dull, whiny men, and thinks that there is always a way out of any situation. If she loves someone, she will be faithful. Aries women are too honest to try leading a double life. They are possessive, jealous, and not only will they not forgive those who are unfaithful, their revenge may be brutal; they know no limits. If you can handle an Aries, don't try to put her in a cage; it is best to give her a long leash. Periodically give her some space – then she will seek you out herself. She is sexual, and believe that anything goes in bed.

Her best partners are a Sagittarius or Leo. A Libra can make a good match after middle age, once both partners have grown wiser and settled down a bit. Gemini and Aquarius are only good partners during the initial phase, when everything is still new, but soon enough, they will lose interest in each other. Scorpios are good matches in bed, but only suitable as lovers.

TAURUS

Taurean women possess qualities that men often dream about, but rarely find in the flesh – they are soft, charming, practical, and reliable – they are very caring and will support their partner in every way. A Taurus is highly sexual, affectionate, and can show a man how to take pleasure to new heights. She is also strong and intense. If she is in love, she will be faithful. But when love fades away, she might find someone else on the side, though she will still fight to save her marriage, particularly if her husband earns good money. A Taurus will not tolerate a man who is disheveled or disorganized, and anyone dating her needs to always be on his toes. She will expect gifts, and likes being taken to expensive restaurants, concerts, and other events. If you argue, try to make the first peace offering, because a Taurus finds it very hard to do so – she might withdraw and ruminate for a long time. Never air your dirty laundry; solve all your problems one-on-one.

Scorpio, Virgo, Capricorn, and Cancer make the best matches. A relationship with an Aries or Sagittarius would be difficult. There is little attraction between a Taurus and a Leo, and initially Libras can make for a good partner in bed, but things will quickly cool off and fall apart. A Taurus and Aquarius make an interesting match – despite the difference in signs, their relationships are often lasting, and almost lifelong.

GEMINI

Gemini women are social butterflies, outgoing, and they easily make friends, and then break off the friendship, if people do not hold their interest. A Gemini falls in love hard, is very creative, and often fantasizes about the object of her affection. She is uninterested in sex without any attachment, loves to flirt, and, for the most part, is not particularly affectionate. She dreams of a partner who is her friend, lover, and a romantic, all at once. A Gemini has no use for a man who brings nothing to the table intellectually. That is a tall order, so Geminis often divorce and marry several times. Others simply marry later in life. Once you have begun a life together, do not try to keep her inside – she needs to travel, explore, socialize, attend events and go to the theater. She cannot tolerate possessive men, so avoid giving her the third degree, and remember that despite her flirtatious and social nature, she is, in fact, faithful – as long as you keep her interested and she is in love. Astrologists believe that Geminis do not know what they need until age 29 or 30, so it is best to hold off on marriage until then.

Leo and Libra make the best matches. A relationship with a Cancer is likely, though complex, and depends solely on the Cancer's affection. A Gemini and Sagittarius can have an interesting, dynamic relationship, but these are two restless signs, which might only manage to get together after ages 40-45, once they have had enough thrills out of life and learned to be patient. Relationships with a Capricorn are very difficult, and almost never happen. The honeymoon stage can be wonderful with a Scorpio, but each partner will eventually go their own way, before ending things. A Gemini and Pisces union can also be very interesting – they are drawn to each other, and can have a wonderful relationship, but after a while, the cracks start to show and things will fall apart. An Aquarius is also not a bad match, but they will have little sexual chemistry.

CANCER

Cancers can be divided into two opposing groups. The first includes a sweet and gentle creature who is willing to dedicate her life to her husband and children. She is endlessly devoted to her husband, especially if he makes a decent living and remains faithful. She views all men as potential husbands, which means it is dangerous to strike up a relationship with her if your intentions are not serious; she can be anxious and clingy, sensitive and prone to crying. It is better to break things to her gently, rather than directly spitting out the cold, hard truth. She wants a man who can be a provider, though she often earns well herself. She puts money away for a rainy day, and knows how to be thrifty, for the sake of others around her, rather than only for herself. She is an excellent cook and capable of building an inviting home for her loved ones. She is enthusiastic in bed, a wonderful wife, and a caring mother.

The second type of Cancer is neurotic, and capable of creating a living hell for those around her. She believes that the world is her enemy, and manages to constantly find new intrigue and machinations.

Another Cancer, Virgo, Taurus, Scorpio, and Pisces make the best matches. A Cancer can often fall in love with a Gemini, but eventually, things will grow complicated, as she will be exhausted by a Gemini's constant mood swings and cheating. A Cancer and Sagittarius will initially have passionate sex, but things will quickly cool off. A relationship with a Capricorn is a real possibility, but only later in life, as while they are young, they are likely to fight and argue constantly. Cancer can also have a relationship with an Aries, but this will not be easy.

LEO

Leos are usually beautiful or charming, and outwardly sexual. And yet, appearances can be deceiving – they are not actually that interested in sex. Leo women want to be the center of attention and men running after them boosts their self-esteem, but they are more interested in their career, creating something new, and success than sex. They often have high-powered careers and are proud of their own achievements. Their partners need to be strong; if a Leo feels a man is weak, she can carry him herself for a while- before leaving him. It is difficult for her to find a partner for life, as chivalrous knights are a dying breed, and she is not willing to compromise. If you are interested in a Leo, take the initiative, admire her, and remember that even a queen is still a woman. Timid men or tightwads need not apply. Leos like to help others, but they don't need a walking disaster in their life. If they are married and in love, they are usually faithful, and petty gossip isn't their thing. Leo women make excellent mothers, and are ready to give their lives to their children. Their negative traits include vanity and a willingness to lie, in order to make themselves look better.

Sagittarius, Aries, and Libra make the best matches. Leos can also have an interesting relationship with a Virgo, though both partners will weaken each other. Life with a Taurus will lead to endless arguments – both signs are very stubborn, and unwilling to give in. Leos and Pisces are another difficult pair, as she will have to learn to be submissive if she wants to keep him around. A relationship with a Capricorn will work if there is a common denominator, but they will have little sexual chemistry. Life with a Scorpio will be turbulent to say the least, and they will usually break up later in life.

VIRGO

Virgo women are practical, clever, and often duplicitous. Marrying one isn't for everyone. She is a neat freak to the point of annoying those around her. She is also an excellent cook, and strives to ensure her children receive the very best by teaching them everything, and preparing them for a bright future. She is also thrifty – she won't throw money around, and, in fact, won't even give it to her husband. She has no time for rude, macho strongmen, and is suspicious of spendthrifts. She will not be offended if you take her to a cozy and modest café rather than an elegant restaurant. Virgos are masters of intrigue, and manage to outperform every other sign of the Zodiac in this regard. Virgos love to criticize everyone and everything; to listen to them, the entire world is simply a disaster and wrong, and only she is the exception to this rule. Virgos are not believed to be particularly sexual, but there are different variations when it comes to this. Rarely, one finds an open-minded Virgo willing to try anything, and who does it all on a grand scale – but she is rather the exception to this general rule.

The best matches for a Virgo are Cancer, Taurus, and Capricorn. She also can get along well with a Scorpio, but will find conflict with Sagittarius. A Pisces will strike her interest, but they will rarely make it down the aisle. She is often attracted to an Aquarius, but they would drive each other up the wall were they to actually marry. An Aries forces Virgo to see another side of life, but here, she will have to learn to conform and adapt.

LIBRA

Female Libras tend to be beautiful, glamorous, or very charming. They are practical, tactical, rational, though they are adept at hiding these qualities behind their romantic and elegant appearance. Libras are drawn to marriage, and are good at imagining the kind of partner they need. They seek out strong, well-off men and are often more interested in someone's social status and bank account than feelings. The object of their affection needs to be dashing, and have a good reputation in society. Libras love expensive things, jewelry, and finery. If they are feeling down, a beautiful gift will instantly cheer them up. They will not tolerate scandal or conflict, and will spend all their energy trying to keep the peace, or at least the appearance thereof. They do not like to air their dirty laundry, and will only divorce in extreme circumstances. They are always convinced they are right and react to any objections as though they have been insulted. Most Libras are not particularly sexual, except those with Venus or the Moon in Scorpio.

Leos, Geminis, and Aquarians make good matches. Libra women are highly attracted to Aries men - this is a real case of opposites attract. They can get along with a Sagittarius, though he will find that Libras are too proper and calm. Capricorn, Pisces, and Cancer are all difficult matches. Things will begin tumultuously with a Taurus, before each partner goes his or her own way.

SCORPIO

Scorpio women may appear outwardly restrained, but there is much more bubbling below the surface. They are ambitious with high self-esteem, but often wear a mask of unpretentiousness. They are the true power behind the scenes, the one who holds the family together, but never talk about it. Scorpios are strong-willed, resilient, and natural survivors. Often, Scorpios are brutally honest, and expect the same out of those around them. They do not like having to conform, and attempt to get others to adapt to them, as they honestly believe everyone will be better off that way. They are incredibly intuitive, and not easily deceived. They have an excellent memory, and can quickly figure out which of your buttons to push. They are passionate in bed, and their temperament will not diminish with age. When she is sexually frustrated, a Scorpio will throw all of her energy into her career or her loved ones. She is proud, categorical, and "if you don't do it right, don't do it at all" is her motto. Scorpio cannot be fooled, and she will not forgive any cheating. Will she cheat herself? Yes! But it will not break up her family, and she will attempt to keep it a secret. Scorpios are usually attractive to men, even if they are not particularly beautiful. They keep a low profile, though they always figure out their partner, and give them some invisible sign. There is also another, selfish type of Scorpio, who will use others for as long as they need them, before unceremoniously casting them aside.

Taurus is a good match; they will have excellent sexual chemistry and understand each other. Scorpio and Gemini are drawn to each other, but are unlikely to stay together long enough to actually get married. Cancer can be a good partner as well, but Cancers are possessive, while Scorpios do not like others meddling in their affairs, though they can later resolve their arguments in bed. Scorpio and Leo are often found together, but their relationship can also be very complicated. Leos are animated and chipper, while Scorpios, who are much deeper and more stubborn, see Leos as not particularly serious or reliable. One good example of this is Bill (a Leo) and Hillary (a Scorpio) Clinton. Virgo can also make a good partner, but when Scorpio seemingly lacks emotions, he will look for them elsewhere. Relationships with Lira are strange and very rare. Scorpio sees Libra as too insecure, and Libra does not appreciate Scorpio's rigidity. Two Scorpios together make an excellent marriage! Sagittarius and Scorpio are unlikely to get together, as she will think he is shallow and rude. If they do manage to get married, Scorpio's drive and persistence is the only thing that will make the marriage last. Capricorn is also not a bad match, and while Scorpio finds Aquarius attractive, they will rarely get married, as they are simply speaking different languages! Things are alright with a Pisces, as both signs are emotional, and Pisces can let Scorpio take the lead when necessary.

SAGITTARIUS

Sagittarius women are usually charming, bubbly, energetic, and have the gift of gab. They are kind, sincere, and love people. They are also straightforward, fair, and very ambitious, occasionally to the point of irritating those around them. But telling them something is easier than not telling them, and they often manage to win over their enemies. Sagittarius tends to have excellent intuition, and she loves to both learn and teach others. She is a natural leader, and loves taking charge at work and at home. Many Sagittarian women have itchy feet, and prefer all kinds of travel to sitting at home. They are not particularly good housewives – to be frank, cooking and cleaning is simply not for them. Their loved ones must learn to adapt to them, but Sagittarians themselves hate any pressure. They are not easy for men to handle, as Sagittarians want to be in charge. Sagittarius falls in love easily, is very sexual and temperamental, and may marry multiple times. Despite outward appearances, Sagittarius is a very lonely sign. Even after she is married with children, she may continue living as if she were alone; you might say she marches to the beat of her own drum. Younger

Sagittarians can be reckless, but as they mature, they can be drawn to religion, philosophy, and the occult.

Aries and Leo make the best matches, as Sagittarius is able to bend to Leo's ways, or at least pretend to. Sagittarians often end up with Aquarians, but their marriages do not tend to be for the long haul. They are attracted to Geminis, but are unlikely to marry one until middle age, when both signs have settled down. Sagittarius and Cancer have incredible sexual chemistry, but an actual relationship between them would be tumultuous and difficult. Capricorn can make a good partner- as long as they are able to respect each other's quirks. Sagittarius rarely ends up with a Virgo, and while she may often meet Pisces, things are unlikely to go very far.

CAPRICORN

Capricorn women are conscientious, reliable, organized, and hard-working. Many believe that life means nothing but work, and live accordingly. They are practical, and not particularly drawn to parties or loud groups of people. But if someone useful will be there, they are sure to make an appearance. Capricorn women are stingy, but not as much as their male counterparts. They are critical of others, but think highly of themselves. Generally, they take a difficult path in life, but thanks to their dedication, perseverance, and willingness to push their own limits, they are able to forge their own path, and by 45 or 50, they can provide themselves with anything they could want. Capricorn women have the peculiarity of looking older than their peers when they are young, and younger than everyone else once they have matured. They are not particularly sexual, and tend to be faithful partners. They rarely divorce, and even will fight until the end, even for a failed marriage. Many Capricorns have a pessimistic outlook of life, and have a tendency to be depressed. They are rarely at the center of any social circle, but are excellent organizers. They have a very rigid view of life and love, and are not interested in a fling, as marriage is the end goal. As a wife, Capricorn is simultaneously difficult and reliable. She is difficult because of her strict nature and difficulty adapting. But she will also take on all the household duties, and her husband can relax, knowing his children are in good hands.

Taurus, Pisces, and Scorpio make good matches. Aries is difficult, once things cool off after the initial honeymoon. When a Capricorn meets another Capricorn, they will be each other's first and last love. Sagittarius isn't a bad match, but they don't always pass the test of time. Aquarius and Capricorn are a difficult match, and rarely found together. Things are too dull with a Virgo, and while Leo can be exciting at first, things will fall apart when he begins showing off. Libra and Aquarius are both difficult partners for Capricorn, and she is rarely found with either of them.

AQUARIUS

A female Aquarius is very different from her male counterparts. She is calm and keeps a cool head, but she is also affectionate and open. She values loyalty above all else, and is unlikely to recover from any infidelity, though she will only divorce if this becomes a chronic trend, and she has truly been stabbed in the back. She is not interested in her partner's money, but rather, his professional success. She is unobtrusive and trusting, and will refrain from listening in on her partner's phone conversations or hacking into his email. With rare exceptions, Aquarian women make terrible housewives. But they are excellent partners in life – they are faithful, never boring, and will not reject a man, even in the most difficult circumstances. Most Aquarians are highly intuitive, and can easily tell the truth from a lie. They themselves only lie in extreme situations, which call for a "white lie" in order to avoid hurting someone's feelings.

Aquarius gets along well with Aries, Gemini, and Libra. She can also have a good relationship with a Sagittarius. Taurus often makes a successful match, though they are emotionally very different; the same goes for Virgo. Aquarius and Scorpio, Capricorn, or Cancer is a difficult match. Pisces can make a good partner as well, as both signs complement each other. Any relationship with a Leo will be tumultuous, but lasting, as Leo is selfish, and Aquarius will therefore have to be very forgiving.

PISCES

Pisces women are very adaptable, musically inclined, and erotic. They possess an innate earthly wisdom, and a good business sense. Pisces often reinvent themselves; they can be emotional, soft, and obstinate, as well as sentimental, at times. Their behavioral changes can be explained by frequent ups and downs. Pisces is charming, caring, and her outward malleability is very attractive to men. She is capable of loving selflessly, as long as the man has something to love. Even if he doesn't, she will try and take care of him until the very end. Pisces' greatest fear is poverty. They are intuitive, vulnerable, and always try to avoid conflict. They love to embellish the truth, and sometimes alcohol helps with this. Rarely, one finds extremely unbalanced, neurotic and dishonest Pisces, who are capable of turning their loved ones' lives into a living Hell!

Taurus, Capricorn, Cancer, and Scorpio make the best matches. She will be greatly attracted to a Virgo, but a lasting relationship is only likely if both partners are highly spiritual. Any union with a Libra is likely to be difficult and full of conflict. Pisces finds Gemini attractive, and they may have a very lively relationship – for a while. Occasionally, Pisces ends up with a Sagittarius, but she will have to fade into the background and entirely submit to him. If she ends up with an Aquarius, expect strong emotional outbursts, and a marriage that revolves around the need to raise their children.

Tatiana Borsch

Made in the USA
Middletown, DE
15 December 2020